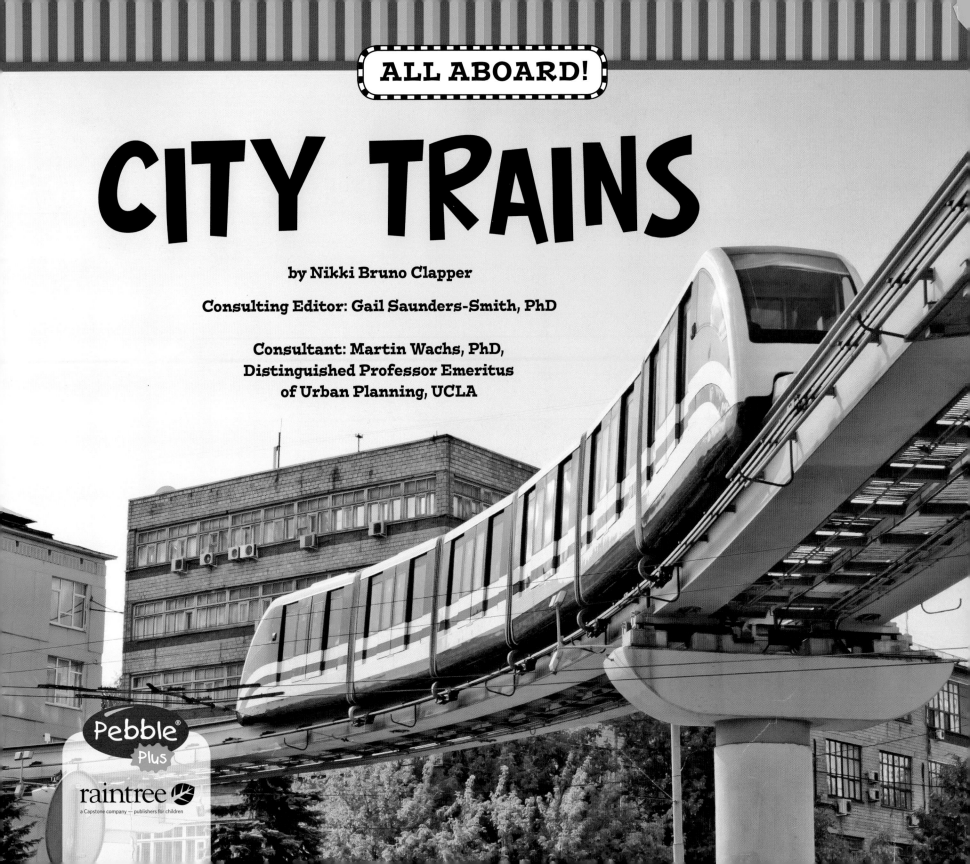

ALL ABOARD!

CITY TRAINS

by Nikki Bruno Clapper

Consulting Editor: Gail Saunders-Smith, PhD

Consultant: Martin Wachs, PhD,
Distinguished Professor Emeritus
of Urban Planning, UCLA

Pebble® Plus

raintree
a Capstone company — publishers for children

Raintree is an imprint of Capstone Global Library Limited, a company incorporated in England and Wales having its registered office at 7 Pilgrim Street, London EC4V 6LB – Registered company number: 6695582

www.raintree.co.uk
myorders@raintree.co.uk
Text © Capstone Global Library Limited 2016
The moral rights of the proprietor have been asserted.

Edited by Nikki Bruno Clapper
Designed by Juliette Peters
Picture research by Jo Miller
Production by Kathy McColley

ISBN 978 1 474 70184 6
19 18 17 16 15
10 9 8 7 6 5 4 3 2 1

British Library Cataloguing in Publication Data
A full catalogue record for this book is available from the British Library.

Acknowledgements
We would like to thank the following for permission to reproduce photographs: Alamy: Agencja Fotograficzna Caro, 11, Chad Ehlers, 9, Directphoto Collection, 7, JLImages, 15, Pegaz, 21, PjrTransport, 19, Rolf Adlercreutz, 5; James P. Rowan, 17; Newscom: Deanpictures/Francis Joseph Dean, 13; Shutterstock: Anton Foltin, cover (train), Denys Prykhodov, cover (phone), oneinchpunch, 2-3, 22-23, PhotoRoman, 1, tovovan, train design element, (throughout)

Every effort has been made to contact copyright holders of material reproduced in this book. Any omissions will be rectified in subsequent printings if notice is given to the publisher.

All the internet addresses (URLs) given in this book were valid at the time of going to press. However, due to the dynamic nature of the internet, some addresses may have changed, or sites may have changed or ceased to exist since publication. While the author and publisher regret any inconvenience this may cause readers, no responsibility for any such changes can be accepted by either the author or the publisher.

Printed in China.

Contents

Out of the darkness

You stand on the busy platform.

A roar fills the dark tunnel.

Then you see a bright light.

The underground train is coming!

Big cities are crowded.

Trains make life easier.

Many people can ride in

each train carriage.

All aboard!

Away from the street

Some city trains travel away from road traffic. They travel above or below the street. This saves space and time.

City trains are built for short trips. The carriages have some seats, but most people need to stand during rush hour.

Most city trains run on electricity and have human drivers. But some trains have no drivers! They are run by computers.

a driverless underground train in Copenhagen, Denmark

Spotlight:
the London Underground

London's famous underground railway is nicknamed the Tube. It has tube-shaped tunnels. But only about half the tracks are underground.

On the street

Trolleys and trams ride

on tracks on streets.

Busy city traffic can

slow them down.

Trolleys and trams are easy
to use. Passengers don't
have to walk up or down
stairs to get to a station.

Spotlight: San Francisco cable cars

The cable cars of San Francisco, California, started running in 1873. Long metal cables pull these railcars up the city's steep hills.

GLOSSARY

cable thick wire or rope

electricity natural force that can be used to make light and heat or to make machines work

passenger person who travels on a plane, train or other vehicle

platform raised, flat surface; people stand on platforms to wait for trains

rush hour time of day when traffic is very heavy, usually when people are going to work or leaving work

train carriage one of the wheeled vehicles that are put together to form a train

tram public transport vehicle that moves on a special pathway

trolley electric street car that runs on tracks and gets power from an overhead wire

FIND OUT MORE

Books

City Train (Stone Arch Readers), Adria F. Klein (Stone Arch Books, 2013)

Trains! (Step into Reading), Susan E. Goodman (Random House, 2012)

Trains (Usborne Beginners), Emily Bone (Usborne, 2011)

Websites

Find out lots of facts about trains:

http://primaryfacts.com/4645/train-facts-for-kids

Learn more about all kinds of trains:

http://easyscienceforkids.com/all-about-trains

INDEX